STEAM ON THE EASTERN AND MIDLAND

A NEW GLIMPSE OF THE 1950s and 1960s

STEAM ON THE EASTERN AND MIDLAND

A NEW GLIMPSE OF THE 1950s and 1960s

DAVID KNAPMAN

Pen & Sword
TRANSPORT

AN IMPRINT OF PEN & SWORD BOOKS LTD.
YORKSHIRE - PHILADELPHIA

First published in Great Britain in 2019 by
Pen and Sword Transport

An imprint of Pen & Sword Books Limited
Yorkshire - Philadelphia

ISBN: 978 1 47389 178 4

Typeset by Aura Technology and Software Services, India
Printed and bound in India by Replika Press Pvt. Ltd.

Pen & Sword Books Limited incorporates the imprints of Atlas, Archaeology, Aviation, Discovery,
Family History, Fiction, History, Maritime, Military, Military Classics, Politics, Select, Transport, True Crime,
Air World, Frontline Publishing, Leo Cooper, Remember When, Seaforth Publishing,
The Praetorian Press, Wharncliffe Local History, Wharncliffe Transport,
Wharncliffe True Crime and White Owl.

For a complete list of Pen & Sword titles please contact

PEN & SWORD BOOKS LIMITED
47 Church Street, Barnsley, South Yorkshire, S70 2AS, England
E-mail: enquiries@pen-and-sword.co.uk
Website: www.pen-and-sword.co.uk

Or
PEN AND SWORD BOOKS
1950 Lawrence Rd, Havertown, PA 19083, USA
E-mail: Uspen-and-sword@casematepublishers.com
Website: www.penandswordbooks.com

CONTENTS

INTRODUCTION

It gives me great pleasure to introduce this book, which is the companion volume to *Steam on the Southern and Western*, published by Pen & Sword in September 2018. In that book, I explained how my interest in railways and railway photography started and to further embellish that information, I have included here pictures of the two cameras that did all the work.

The Brownie Box camera was used by my father before the Second World War and by me to capture some of my first railway scenes in the late 1950s. This camera used to have a small wooden wedge slotted in against the shutter lever to prevent double exposures. Woe betide you if the wedge was lost!

Then in 1959, following a school entrance scholarship success, I was given a 35mm Agfa Silette Vario camera, which took the majority of my black and white photographs. The two hundredths of a second shutter speed helped enormously in taking pictures of moving trains, but it was a far cry from the digital cameras of today. Also, I had to guess the light exposure, as funds would not stretch to a light meter.

In April 1960, my family moved from Surrey to Herongate, near Brentwood, in Essex. This move opened new horizons, as the lines from Liverpool Street and Fenchurch Street were in cycling distance and once schooldays were past, the train service to London facilitated reasonably easy access to London Termini and beyond. Holidays also took us further afield, with Yorkshire being a favourite destination.

In the same format as *Southern and Western*, this book will have chapters covering different locations in the Eastern and London Midland regions, with photographs of branch and main line trains as well as locations of interest and some,

where trains run no more. Very few of these photographs have been published before.

In concluding this introduction, I am keen to say how pleasurable it is working with the Pen and Sword team. I have found kind support and patience in producing my books and I am most grateful and encouraged by that help.

Grateful thanks are due to Jenifer and David Alison, who have taken time to carefully read and comment on the scripts of both books. I am very appreciative of that help.

So, if you enjoy reading this book, do think about putting your own memories forward to Pen and Sword; you will enjoy the hard work and the experience!

David Knapman,
Woburn
September 2019

PART ONE
EASTERN REGION

CHAPTER 1

PATELEY BRIDGE

Pateley Bridge station was the terminus of a North Eastern Railway branch which ran from Nidd Junction on the Harrogate to Ripon line, for 11½ miles to Pateley Bridge. The branch opened to traffic in 1862. Passenger traffic became very sparse after the Second World War, ceasing in March 1951. Goods traffic lasted until October 1964 and included construction items for reservoir projects in Upper Nidderdale. In August 1959, we were staying in Pateley Bridge for our first Yorkshire holiday and as I looked out of the hotel window at lunch time, steam suddenly appeared at the end of the hotel garden. On 4 August, I managed to escape the discipline of lunch to photograph an ex-LNER J39 0-6-0 64861, as it shunted in the station yard.

Starbeck allocated 'J39' 0-6-0 64861 is backing wagons into the yard at Pateley Bridge. Note the signal box is out of use with its windows smashed, although the name board is still present. The water column has an elegant swan neck, the water being supplied from the large tank seen above 64861.

64861 peers smokily over the wall dividing the railway yard from the riverside path. Above the wagons, the station building can be seen with its stepped end wall stonework attributed to Thomas Prosser, whilst on the right is the substantial goods shed. The fireman is taking an interest in my activities.

Pateley Bridge station from the hillside overlooking the railway, providing another view of the architecture and layout. 8 August 1959.

CHAPTER 2

YORK RAILWAY MUSEUM

In 1959, the large exhibits of the York Railway Museum were housed in a building known as the Queen Street Section, about 250 yards from the main station entrance. Admission cost 6d. The railway museum leaflet stated that 'nowhere else in the World can be seen assembled under one roof full-size locomotives, all of which have been the wonder-engines of their day'. In contrast to the National Railway Museum (NRM) today, there were few exhibits in 1959. Photography in the old museum was far from easy, but here are some scenes from 6 August 1959.

Ivatt large 'Atlantic' 251 peers round a poster depicting James Ramsbottom, who worked for the London and North Western Railway in expanding Crewe works. 251 had its last run in September 1953, hauling the *Plant Centenarian* with 'Small Atlantic' 990 *Henry Oakley*. At the date of this photograph, that was only six years before.

Great Northern Railway 4-2-2 No 1 of 1870, with eight-foot driving wheels, is hiding behind a North Eastern Railway tender belonging to 2-4-0 1463 and London, Brighton and South Coast Railway 0-4-2 *Gladstone* can be seen behind No 1. The GNR 4-2-2 was permitted to run on the preserved Great Central Railway in 1982 and I had the privilege of riding behind this elegant machine.

To the right of this picture, the driving wheel of No 1 dominates the scene, whilst NER 4-4-0 1621 of 1893 completes the picture. 1621 took part in the 1895 railway races to the North.

CHAPTER 3

YORK STATION AND SHED

Staying with the Yorkshire theme, it is appropriate to visit York station and show photographs from various occasions. The splendid station building covered platforms which accommodated trains from the North, London, Scarborough, Hull, Harrogate, Leeds and further afield. The curving train shed roof is credited to William Peachey and this station was opened on 25 June 1877, succeeding two previous stations in York. The amalgamation of three lines promoted by George Hudson led to the formation of the North Eastern Railway and eventually to the provision of the 795 foot long curved train shed, supported by cast iron columns and wrought iron roofing ribs. Whether visiting York station in steam days or modern times, the station remains awe inspiring.

York North Shed, as it was originally known, opened in 1878. When the LNER took over the shed at the Grouping, the shed had four roundhouses. War damage after an air raid caused the shed to be rebuilt as a straight shed with two roundhouses, and the 70 foot turntable was also repaired. This shed became part of the NRM in 1975.

Dull weather persists and the locomotive is dirty, but Gateshead's single chimney 'A3' 4-6-2 60040 *Cameronian* is arriving with an express from the North. To the left of the picture, locomotives rest outside the shed. 6 August 1959.

The weather may be dull, but clean 'Jubilee' 4-6-0 45717 *Dauntless*, from Bank Hall shed, is a delight!
Hauling a train of ex-LMS coaches, the 'Jubilee' is probably on a Newcastle to Liverpool working. 45717 was
withdrawn in October 1963. 6 August 1959.

At the south end of the station, a Wilson Worsdell 1898 designed 'J72' 0-6-0 tank 68687 is on empty stock
duties with the splendid station canopy overseeing its activities. 6 August 1959.

You might be forgiven for thinking that the LMS had taken over York station. Here York shedded 'Jinty' 0-6-0T 47448 is also attending to empty stock. Note the oval white windows of the Thompson coach behind 47448. 6 August 1959.

Gresley 'A4' pacific 60033 *Seagull* is leaving York with a northbound express. 60033 is a King's Cross Top Shed engine, which was withdrawn only a few months later in December 1962. The first coach is another Thompson vehicle and the usual gallery is watching the departure. 7 August 1962.

A southbound fast freight is about to thread its way through York station, headed by Gresley 'V2' 2-6-2 60924, a Doncaster resident. It is astride Waterworks Junction where the East Coast Main Line meets the line to Scarborough, disappearing to the right of the picture. 7 August 1962.

This southbound van train has been checked outside York and the pilot engine '5MT' 4-6-0 45243 is starting away strongly in protest at the delay. The 'Jubilee' train engine 45695 *Minotaur* has yet to respond. 45243 is from Crewe North shed whilst 45695 is allocated to Farnley Junction, so it would be interesting to know how this duty enabled the locomotives to return to their depots. 7 August 1962.

Not only is the Gresley pacific filthy, but burnt as well. The smokebox door shows signs of hard work or neglect or probably both. Heaton based 'A3' 4-6-2 60088 *Book Law* is approaching York with a southbound express; a Gresley brake coach is at the head of the train. 7 August 1962.

A railtour from London to Darlington, the *London & North Eastern Flier* on 2 May 1964, included a stopover at York where a shed visit was part of the itinerary. Looking inside the shed building (now part of the NRM) a group of York shedded locomotives is revealed as they huddle round the turntable. From left to right are: 'A1' 4-6-2 60150 *Willbrook*; 'A1' 4-6-2 60121 *Silurian*; 'V2' 2-6-2 60929 and 'B1' 4-6-0 61049. The next three pictures were taken on the same occasion.

Outside the shed, a Gresley 'V2' 2-6-2 is moving slowly down the yard. 60877 lasted until February 1966.

York's smartly turned out 'B1' 4-6-0 61031 *Reedbuck* is receiving attention before its next duty; a bright light in the mist and gloom. The 'B1' was withdrawn in October 1964, only a few months later, but not before 61031 was involved in railtour traffic.

Wilson Worsdell designed 'J27' 0-6-0 65844 is shunting in York shed yard, whilst a crew member takes interest in the shed visitors. This venerable machine has the later British Railways tender emblem.

RIPON

Ripon station was on the line from the junction with the East Coast Main Line (ECML) at Northallerton on which trains could reach Harrogate, York, Leeds and Doncaster. At the time, the line was a useful diversionary route for the ECML if engineering works were required. Unfortunately, the line and station fell victim to Dr Beeching's cuts. The station opened on 1 June 1848, closed to passengers in March 1967 and completely in September 1969. Passenger traffic included Leeds to Northallerton trains, Liverpool to Newcastle services and the *Queen of Scots* for King's Cross and Glasgow. Freight traffic was plentiful, but my visit must have coincided with a quiet period, although this did not detract from the interest of the location.

On a rather dull day, 'J39' 0-6-0 64857 is heading south, light engine, through Ripon station. The 'J39' has an ex-North Eastern Railway tender, probably from a 'D20' 4-4-0. A 'WD' 2-8-0 90059 waits in the yard for a path southwards. Another 'J39''s tender, the flush sided variety, is being refilled at the right hand water column. Under the canopy, a maintenance man looks in a precarious position, whilst two engine crew walk down the platform, bantering with the 'J39''s fireman. In the background, left, two men are loading a lorry. It is all happening! Note the 'tucked up' water hose above the northbound running line. 13 August 1959.

The 'WD' 2-8-0 90059, mentioned previously, is released from the yard to take its ballast train southwards. 90059 is allocated to Frodingham. Note the extensive slate roof of the adjacent building. The Ripon totem would be in North Eastern tangerine colour. 13 August 1959.

CHAPTER 5

KING'S CROSS

Opened in 1852, Cubitt's terminus for the Great Northern Railway was a very striking building, which in steam days was no doubt derided for being a smoky den, but it had a special atmosphere of its own, attracting generations of enthusiasts to its platforms. There had always been a number of other buildings at the front of the terminus, cluttering the symmetrical view of the station frontage. King's Cross was threatened with redevelopment, but thankfully has been restored to the attractive building it is today. I paid numerous visits to King's Cross, sometimes without a camera as film could not always be afforded. So, the 'W1' 4-6-4 60700 and 'B2' 4-6-0s 61603 and 61615 escaped the lens. Worse still, on 11 June 1962, I had no camera on a day trip to Hitchin when ex-works 'A3' 60103 *Flying Scotsman* was at the head of my train, with class mate 60108 *Gay Crusader* in charge for the return. 'N2's and 'J50's were 'too common' to be captured on film, but let us look at some of the other visitors to the 'Cross' in this chapter.

Named 'B1' 4-6-0 61026 *Ourebi*, a Lincoln resident, has brought a train, possibly from Cleethorpes, into King's Cross. It is now backing out of the station to go on shed for servicing. Note there is a 'J50' standing near the entrance to Gasworks Tunnel. The signal box looks grime encrusted as usual. 12 September 1959.

On a dull January day, double chimney 'A3' 4-6-2 60111 *Enterprise* is in the locomotive yard adjacent to the station platforms. 60111 is facing up to the competition in the form of a Brush type 2 diesel. Trough deflectors would not appear on 60111 until April 1962 and it would travel 1.9 million miles before withdrawal in December 1962. 5 January 1961.

My favourite trick is to miss the arrival of famous locomotives and discover them at the bufferstops, where light is harder to find. Top Shed resident 'A3' 60103 *Flying Scotsman* has arrived from the North and is not attracting special attention as it does today. It is clean and awaits trough smoke deflectors. 5 January 1961.

On a wet April day, 'A3' pacific 60103 *Flying Scotsman* is at the head of a northbound express at King's Cross. The fireman has a task in mind, whilst the driver is climbing into the cab. 60103 looks in good Top Shed shape. 3 April 1961.

Classmate 'A3' 4-6-2 60109 *Hermit* awaits clearance to go on shed and she is newly fitted with trough deflectors. In the background, sister engine 60110 *Robert The Devil* awaits departure. 60110 will wait another seven months for the new deflectors. Both these 'A3's achieved over 2 million miles and were Top Shed residents. 3 April 1961.

Immingham allocated
'Britannia' 4-6-2
70041 *Sir John
Moore* is departing
King's Cross with the
4.15pm Cleethorpes
express. It is about
to pass the eight
miles per hour speed
restriction sign...such
a precise requirement.
7 August 1961.

Long term Haymarket
resident Gresley
'A4' pacific 60024
Kingfisher is
approaching the
terminus with the
up *Elizabethan*.
60024 looks as if it is
starting its journey,
not ending it, such
is its appearance.
7 August 1961.

Thompson 'B1' 4-6-0 61190 of Immingham shed is awaiting departure with an afternoon Cleethorpes service. The driver is leaning from the cab to see all is well, whilst flower boxes rest on a platform trolley. The locomotive has electric lighting supplemented by oil lamps. The design of coach on the adjacent track complements the locomotive. 7 August 1961.

Grantham's 'A3' 4-6-2 60047 *Donovan* is moving very gently in the locomotive yard by the platforms. Named after the 1889 Derby and St. Leger winner, *Donovan* travelled over 2 million miles for its owners before retiring in April 1963. 7 August 1961.

This photograph is outside the specific scope of this book, but it was taken by the Brownie Box camera mentioned in the introduction. Taken by my father on his seventeenth birthday, 2 August 1930, this photograph shows Ivatt large 'Atlantic' 4404 standing in the locomotive yard just as *Donovan* did 31 years later. 4404 ran to time with a train of 17 coaches, 585 tons gross between Grantham and York in 1936, reaching 77mph at Retford in the process. A superb effort.

Returning to the correct era, 'A1' pacific 60141 *Abbotsford,* a Copley Hill engine at this time, waits to leave King's Cross with a Leeds express. The smoky Gasworks Tunnel beckons beyond the eight mph speed limit sign. 22 August 1962.

CHAPTER 6

THE LONDON & NORTH EASTERN FLIER

On Saturday, 2 May 1964, the Gresley Society sponsored a special train which travelled from King's Cross to Darlington, in view of the imminent withdrawal of Gresley pacifics from the ECML. An engine change occurred at Doncaster and there was a two hour layover at York, enabling a visit to York Shed (See Chapter Three). Arrival at Darlington North Road at 2.20pm provided an excellent opportunity to see the train locomotive being serviced, as well as other Gresley pacifics on shed. There was also a conducted tour of the locomotive works and a visit to the North Road 'Scrap Yard'. The motive power for the train was 'A3' 60106 *Flying Fox* from King's Cross to Doncaster and return and 'A3' 4472 *Flying Scotsman*, then owned by Alan Pegler, from Doncaster to Darlington and return. To complement the locomotives, the coaching stock was entirely Gresley vehicles weighing in total 320 tons. Both locomotives were worked hard, wherever possible, culminating in a thrilling run down Stoke Bank by 60106 on the return run, with the speed reaching just over 100mph, before signals required a rapid brake application. A report by a footplate rider at the time expressed how well the 41-year-old 60106 was riding, a very fitting farewell to a grand pacific. 60106 was withdrawn from New England shed on 26 December 1964 having run in the region of 2.7 million miles.

New England's 'A3' 4-6-2 60106 *Flying Fox* is backing down towards the train at King's Cross. The grand old lady has been well prepared on shed.

60106 has arrived at Peterborough having reached 90mph near Hitchin. The locomotive change to 4472 *Flying Scotsman* will take place at Doncaster. 60106's return was largely in the dark when the 100+mph occurred at Little Bytham. I had always been under the impression that the top speed was about 96mph before being checked by signals. 51 years later I discovered the information about the 'ton' in Peter Coster's book *90 Years On, the New Book of the A3 Pacifics* on the penultimate page. My only 100mph with steam.

'A3' 4472 has arrived at Darlington North Road, destination of the outward journey, having run a number of miles, after York, at well over 80mph.

4472 is in glorious LNER apple green livery in Darlington shed yard. Alan Pegler is standing by the smokebox door cleaning the top hand rail.

Two Gresley pacifics in steam. 4472 has sister engine 60045 *Lemberg* for company at Darlington.

Darlington allocated 'A3' 60045 *Lemberg* is stand by locomotive for the day in the event of a failure requiring replacement power. The engine's lamps are on the cab footsteps.

Another Darlington 'A3' takes a bow. 60036 *Colombo* is on the move, with 4472 resting in the background.

Ready to go! 4472 *Flying Scotsman* has been serviced and stands outside the Darlington shed building.

Also in the shed yard was Darlington's 'B1' 4-6-0 61304, awaiting its next task.

West Hartlepool's 'Q6' 0-8-0 63410 is resting at Darlington after exertions that have burned its smokebox door, and priming could be the cause of decoration to the chimney.

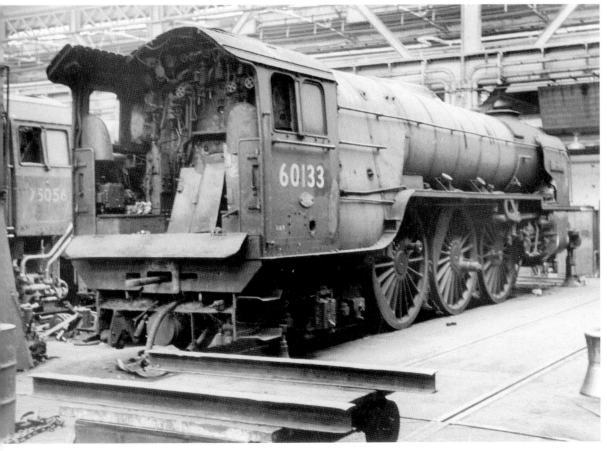

A guided tour of Darlington works revealed Copley Hill's 'A1' 4-6-2 60133 *Pommern* under repair, with Stoke's '4MT' 4-6-0 75056 receiving attention too.

York's 'B1' 4-6-0 61256 is under repair, minus boiler, with a 'V2' 2-6-2 behind.

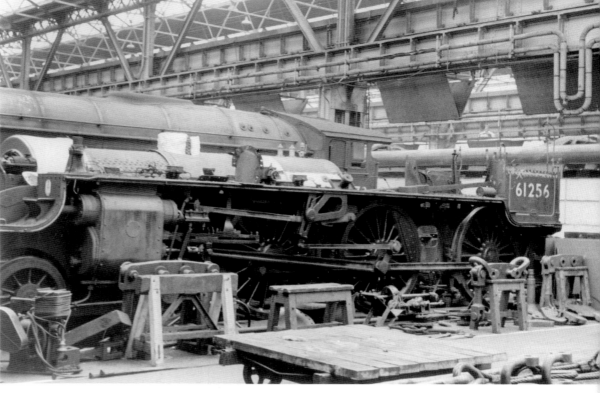

Some interesting and surprising engines were in the 'Scrap Road'. 'B1' 4-6-0 61038 *Blacktail* was withdrawn in May 1964.

North Eastern Railway 'J21' 0-6-0 65033 had been withdrawn in April 1962. This locomotive is still with us, awaiting restoration.

Sister 'J21' 65099 had been withdrawn in November 1961 and looked the worse for wear.

It was very disappointing to see two 'A4' 4-6-2s in the scrap line. 60011 *Empire of India* was withdrawn in June 1964.

Both 'A4's had open 'cod's mouths' and here is Gateshead's 60020 *Guillemot* having been taken out of service in March 1964. A sad end to two speedy pacifics. Fortunately, we still had the prospect of fast running to come behind the two 'A3's on the return run of *The London & North Eastern Flier*.

CHAPTER 7

LIVERPOOL STREET

Liverpool Street is in the east of the City of London and can be described as the gateway to East Anglia. Great Eastern lines had originally terminated at Bishopsgate, but this terminus was found to be unsatisfactory, leading to the opening of Liverpool Street in 1874. Main line trains were worked to Cambridge, Colchester, Ipswich, Norwich, Cromer, Yarmouth, Clacton and Parkeston Quay, with intensive suburban services to Enfield, Palace Gates, Chingford, Chelmsford and Southend. By 1894, Liverpool Street had eighteen platforms and before 1914 was handling 200,000 passengers daily. In the early 1950s, electrification of the lines to Shenfield had been completed and further electrification of all the suburban lines followed. Steam was eliminated from Liverpool Street in September 1962. This chapter will show some of the locomotives that could be found at this atmospheric terminus.

A change of school meant that I was travelling between Surrey and Brentwood in Essex. Fortunately, I had my camera on 12 September 1959, to capture Norwich based 'Britannia' 4-6-2 70003 *John Bunyan* backing on to the turntable at Liverpool Street with a crew member making sure that 70003 is on the turntable. The customary young audience observes the action.

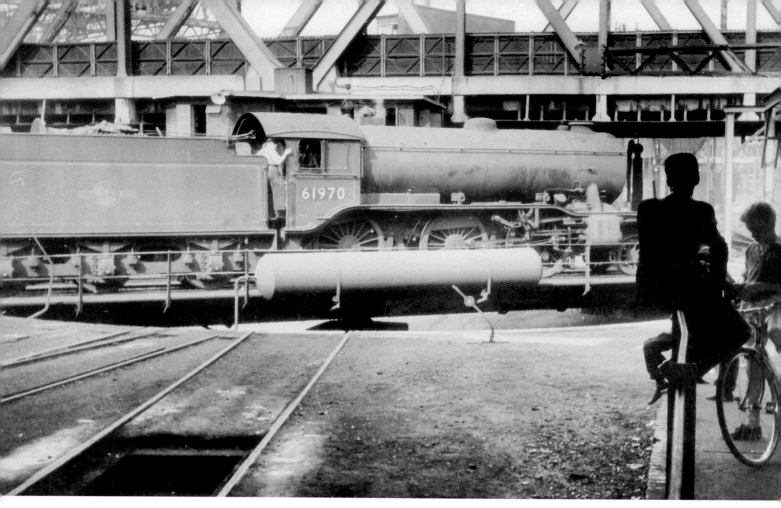

Norwich's Gresley 'K3' 2-6-0 61970 is in mid-turn on the turntable. This must have been a long run for this class of locomotive, not known for being the most comfortable riders. 12 September 1959.

I believe this Gresley three cylinder 'B17' 4-6-0 61668 *Bradford City* was based at Colchester at this time. This was a fortunate chance to photograph a 'Sandy' and 61668 had been withdrawn by July 1960. Note the Westinghouse air pump and the 'footballer' style nameplate. 12 September 1959.

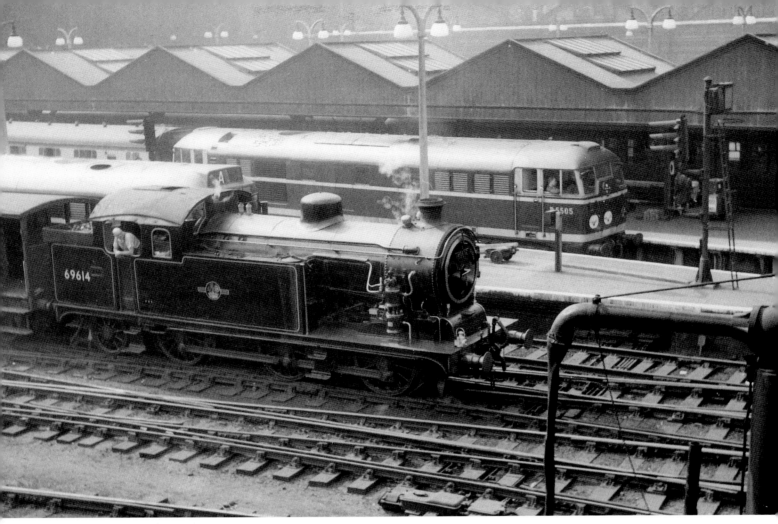

Reflecting the locomotives that operated the 'Jazz Trains', the intensive suburban trains to Enfield, Palace Gates and Chingford, A.J. Hill designed 'N7' 0-6-2T 69614 is acting as station pilot on 12 September 1959.

The taxi rank ramp at Liverpool Street provided a good grandstand for photography, but you had to ignore the overhead wires. Here 'Britannia' pacific 70002 *Geoffrey Chaucer* has a full head of steam ready to take out an eastbound express. 15 August 1960.

Stratford shed kept the two Liverpool Street Station pilots in exemplary condition. 'N7' 69614 is shown above, whilst Holden 'J69' 0-6-0T 68619 is on duty on 31 August 1960. This splendid machine was built in 1904 and left service in November 1961.

After a day's 'gricing' at Waterloo and Vauxhall, the return journey home produced 'Britannia' 4-6-2 70009 *Alfred The Great* waiting for work at Liverpool Street. I am not sure whether the driver welcomed the camera. 8 September 1961.

We travelled en famille by car from Brentwood to Liverpool Street to witness the arrival of the last scheduled steam service to use the terminus. Stratford shed's shining 'B1' 4-6-0 61156 stands in front of an admiring audience, having brought in an express from Parkeston Quay. The end of an era. 9 September 1962.

CHAPTER 8

EAST ANGLIAN MAIN LINE

I n the early 1960s, the main line from Liverpool Street to Colchester was within cycling distance and family motoring expeditions, so this chapter will cover some locations between Ingatestone and Ipswich.

The main line from Liverpool Street to Norwich was constructed in stages by the Eastern Counties Railway and the Eastern Union Railway and their predecessors. It was not until 1850 that a complete journey could be made between London and Norwich.

The 1950s and early 1960s became the era of the 'Britannias' which enabled marked accelerations of services for the Great Eastern Lines. Steam at Liverpool Street finished in September 1962 and so some of the traffic included the movement of electric units to and from Ilford to the Clacton branch.

The locations for this chapter will be Ingatestone, a level crossing near Boreham, east of Chelmsford, Kelvedon station, Colchester station and Ipswich station.

On 31 March 1962, 'Britannia' 4-6-2 70003 *John Bunyan* is speeding through Ingatestone with the Railway Correspondence & Travel Society's *Great Eastern Steam Commemorative Special* train for Norwich. The stock appears to be mostly Gresley and Thompson vehicles.

Now moving east of Chelmsford to an occupation crossing in the vicinity of Boreham on 22 August 1960, we find a useful cycle location for photographing trains in action. Modernisation was in the air, but steam still had work to do. Looking east, Colchester's 'B1' 4-6-0 61311 is at the head of a westbound van train. Note the oil lamps above the electric lights on the bufferbeam.

'Britannia' pacific 70013 *Oliver Cromwell* is marching an up express past the occupation crossing. New concrete troughs adorn the lineside in preparation for replacing the telegraph pole route. 70013 is a well-known preserved main line performer at the time of writing.

Clear views of down trains were available as well, but it was a pity that the adjacent crossing house was neglected. Another Norwich based 'Britannia', 70030 *William Wordsworth,* is gathering pace after the Chelmsford stop.

At this time, electric units were moved between Ilford and the electrified lines from Colchester to Clacton. Two four coach units are heading eastwards powered by March shed's 'K1' 2-6-0 62038, also carrying oil lamps above the electric lamp system.

Another electric unit is being returned to Ilford, headed by A.J. Hill designed 'J20' 0-6-0 64679. These locomotives were rebuilt with 'B12/1' boilers with round topped fireboxes.

Looking east again, 'B1' 4-6-0 61336 is heading an up express from Clacton. This 'B1' was shedded at Parkeston. Note the rather striking telegraph pole route, which will soon disappear under modernisation.

Last but not least at this location. 'Britannia' 70036 *Boadicea* is thundering past the level crossing, hauling an up express, with a Gresley coach immediately behind the tender. Many of the express trains at this time included Gresley brakes or buffet cars, which helped their survival on preserved lines today.

Kelvedon station was the next port of call during a parental motoring expedition on 16 August 1960. The view from the footbridge was lengthy in both directions and Stratford's 'B1' 4-6-0 61119 is rattling through the station with a down express. The signal box is visible above the up line canopy.

Kelvedon's up home signal is expectant, whilst the view portrays the junction with the Tollesbury branch, dropping away from the main line and then curving to the south. The branch was open for freight traffic to Tiptree for the jam factory. This view is looking towards Feering Halt.

The up home signal at Kelvedon has cleared the way for 'J20' 64679 working an empty stock electric unit heading for Ilford. This seemed to be 64679's ongoing job; it is crossing the turnout to the Tollesbury branch. 16 August 1960.

Fortunately, my railway enthusiast father decided I needed to visit Colchester station on the same day. The weather is grey, the locomotive filthy and 'Britannia' 4-6-2 70000 *Britannia* seems to be blending with the dirty engine shed as it leaves the Colchester stop for Norwich.

Further movements of electric stock were taking place at Colchester as 'N7' 0-6-2T 69730 is moving up to adverse signals. Note the 40mph speed restriction for the curve through the station.

Stratford shed's 'K1' 62053, in filthy external condition, is waiting for signals to clear before it can move another electric unit eastwards.

An up Norwich express headed by 'Britannia' pacific 70038 *Robin Hood* is approaching Colchester station past Colchester Junction signal box. Note the overhead catenary for the Clacton and Walton lines. The electrification 'gap' between Colchester and Shenfield required steam haulage of units for maintenance at Ilford.

Moving now to Ipswich, the station there was opened in June 1846 by the Eastern Union Railway, when the first train left Ipswich to reach Colchester. The up fast line ran as a middle road through the station, as shown by 'Britannia' pacific 70037 *Hereward The Wake* about to thread a path between two Brush diesels and make a stop at the up platform. The scenes at Ipswich are dated 9 September 1960.

An up train had at the rear a wooden-bodied inspection saloon bearing a Great Eastern Railway builder's plate and similarly marked axleboxes.

An eastbound express enters Ipswich station, headed by 'Britannia' 4-6-2 70040 *Clive of India* returning to its Norwich base.

'Britannia' pacific 70001 *Lord Hurcomb* is starting a London express from Ipswich and will be about to enter Ipswich tunnel, which provides the route through Stoke Hill.

CHAPTER 9

THE ALDEBURGH BRANCH

A friend had invited me to stay at Aldeburgh in September 1960 and it provided an opportunity to record the stations of the branch from Saxmundham to Aldeburgh. The branch services had commenced in April 1860. The timetable in the 1960s provided seven trains each way, but there were no Sunday trains. On 12 September 1966, passenger services ceased and the branch as far as Sizewell was retained for construction traffic for the Sizewell B power station. Garrett's Agricultural Machinery works at Leiston contributed to the freight revenues. The branch is presently disused but may see construction traffic again if Sizewell is further developed.

From Saxmundham station platform, 'B1' 4-6-0 61045 of Norwich shed has arrived with the afternoon pick up freight, bound for Ipswich. Here the 'B1' is shunting a wagon towards the goods shed, before resuming its journey. The Aldeburgh line branched to the right, well beyond the station platforms. 7 September 1960.

Here is Leiston station looking towards Aldeburgh, with the lines to Garrett's works curving off to the right. Note the lower quadrant signal beyond the signal box. 8 September 1960.

This view of Thorpeness station is looking towards Saxmundham. Ancient coach bodies serve as station buildings. The telegraph pole route looks somewhat fragile. Curiously this station does not appear in the fifth edition of the *Ian Allan Pre-Grouping Atlas*. 8 September 1960.

This is the terminus at Aldeburgh, with its overall roof. At the time of this visit, the line was worked by DMUS. The little platform building sports a crop of hollyhocks, and a splendid gas lamp, complete with mantles, is clearly visible. 7 September 1960.

CHAPTER 10

AUDLEY END

The Audley End to Bartlow branch via Saffron Walden was opened in 1866, its main purpose being to bring rail transport to Saffron Walden, then a rail-less town of reasonable size. Traffic did not come up to expectation, in spite of opening Acrow Halt to serve the business of that name. Dr Beeching's axe fell on this line and by the end of 1964 all services had ceased. My visit to the branch took place on 13 August 1960, when the service was operated by a German railbus.

Saffron Walden station looking west towards Audley End. Steam age equipment is still obvious and the semaphore signal has a wooden post, whilst the smoke besmirched goods shed is beyond the station.

'K3' 2-6-0 61862 enters Audley End main line station, heading for the staggered platform for up trains, where it will connect with the railbus service. The Gresley brake is prominent at the front of this train. Note the wagon turntable to the right of 61862.

This is the branch platform at Audley End with the railbus arriving from Saffron Walden. Two lower quadrant semaphore signals complete the scene.

CHAPTER 11

CAMBRIDGE

A visit to Cambridge station on 13 April 1961 found very little through traffic of interest, but there were numerous movements to and from the locomotive shed and in the shed yard, which helpfully was adjacent to the long single platform of Cambridge station. The locomotives depicted here were Cambridge residents apart from 61096 and 62040, which belonged to March shed. Cambridge shed closed to steam in June 1962 and all the ex-LNER locomotives shown here had been withdrawn by September 1962, but BR built 62040 lasted until January 1965.

Ex-G.E.R. 'J15' 0-6-0 65478 is about to make a foray into the yard to shunt some unsuspecting trucks.

Resident 'B1' 4-6-0 61301 is at rest by the wall dividing the platform from the running shed.

'K3' 2-6-0 61834 has woken from its sojourn in the shed and is raising steam to deal with some serious work.

Whilst all is quiet on the main running lines, 61834 has an audience whilst shunting 'WD' 2-8-0 90501, Ivatt '2MT' 2-6-0 46465, and 'J17' 0-6-0 65578, an awkward load in a somewhat restricted area. Note the lower quadrant bracket signal to the right of the picture.

'K1' 2-6-0 62040 has emerged to have its tender replenished, with a crew member watching the water level rise.

Peace at last for 'B1' 61301 with sister locomotive 61096 sitting alongside. It looks as though the sun might be shining through the smoke haze.

CHAPTER 12

LCGB GREAT EASTERN SUBURBAN RAIL TOUR

The Locomotive Club of Great Britain ran an excellent rail tour of East London suburban lines reaching Palace Gates, Chingford, North Woolwich and Ongar. Stratford, with all its connecting routes, enabled access between all the various destinations. The train comprised three BR mark one coaches and the motive power was provided by 'N7' 0-6-2T 69621, the last Great Eastern locomotive to be built, and 'J15' 0-6-0 65476. The 'J15' gained access to the Ongar line via Leyton and a link north of Stratford. This trip took place on 7 April 1962, with the weather dull as usual.

'N7' 0-6-2T 69621, sporting the LCGB headboard, is completing the run round of the special train at Palace Gates on the branch from Seven Sisters.

Minus headboard, 69621 has uncoupled from the train at Chingford, where engines will be changed. Note the Westinghouse air pump and the use of discs for the headcode.

'J15' 65476 has been coupled to the train at Chingford by the crew member emerging from the rear of the tender, whilst the headboards are about to adorn the front of the locomotive.

Although the Central Line tube trains still ran to Ongar, 'J15' 65476 has found a path to arrive at that terminus, with the tour participants gathering on the platform. The station is in use today by the Epping Ongar Railway.

CHAPTER 13

'B12' AND 'J15'

The last surviving 'B12' 4-6-0 61572 and 'J15' 65462 were destined for preservation, but at times it seemed a matter of conjecture whether these two venerable engines would reach new owners. During that period, the 'B12' worked the legendary *M&GN Wandering 1500* railtour on 5 October 1963, travelling from Broad Street via Hitchin, Bedford,

Northampton, Blisworth and Fenny Compton to reach Stratford upon Avon. The return route was via Leamington Spa, Rugby and Watford to reach Broad Street, and the 'Old Girl' performed beyond expectations during the day. The 'B12' and the 'J15' were subsequently stored in Bow shed, pending their preservation. Here are some memories of that superb excursion.

61572 is well into its journey and is running round its train at Blisworth prior to going forward to Towcester and Fenny Compton. Two crew members are watching the photographers carefully. Note steam is escaping from the Westinghouse pump. The 'B12' gave a good account of itself on the climb out of Blisworth and indeed for the rest of this memorable tour.

At the start of the railtour, here is the 'B12' which has been taken out of storage to power the *M&GN Wandering 1500* on 5 October 1963. 61572 is at Broad Street carrying train code 1X69, but has yet to receive the headboard. Huge thanks were due to David Butcher who oversaw the day's footplate activity to ensure the success of a railtour which is much respected still.

After the excitement of the *Wandering 1500* tour, 'B12' 4-6-0 61572 and 'J15' 0-6-0 65462 were placed in store at Devons Road, Bow shed pending a move to a preservation site. Here the two locomotives await their fate on 14 March 1964. Note the stovepipe chimney and tender cab of the 'J15'.

'J15' 0-6-0 65462 at Devons Road, Bow. 14 March 1964.

CHAPTER 14

LONDON, TILBURY & SOUTHEND LINES

In the 1960s, the LT&S lines were treated as being part of the Eastern Region of British Railways, hence reference to them here in spite of the preponderance of ex-LMS motive power. To reflect the use of the Brownie Box camera, I have included here two of my father's photographs, which show some interesting LMS locomotives of the 1930s albeit outside the theme of this book. This LMS oriented chapter will serve as a useful link to Part Two of this book which will cover the London Midland Region of British Railways.

Ex-LT&SR 4-4-2T 2103 is ready to leave Leigh-on-Sea station with a Southend stopping train which had travelled via Tilbury from Fenchurch Street on 24 August 1930. 2103 was originally number 62 *Camden Road* and was withdrawn in March 1951.

My father was 17 when he took this picture on 24 August 1930. Class '3F' 0-6-0 3261 is at Leigh-on-Sea on a holiday excursion train to Southend. 31 years later, I was able to see '4F' 0-6-0s powering Southend excursions, so not much had changed in that time!

Back to the 1960s and Stanier 3-cylinder '4MT' 2-6-4T 42513 is running fast down Laindon bank towards West Horndon station with a Southend to Fenchurch Street train. 2 September 1960.

The overhead catenary is in place, but steam is still in charge as Stanier 3-cylinder '4MT' 2-6-4T 42529 slows for the West Horndon stop, with a Southend train. 3 August 1961.

Kentish Town's Stanier '5MT' 4-6-0 44846 is heading a tidy rake of ex-LMS excursion coaches past West Horndon, originating from St Pancras and heading for Southend. 44846 lasted until January 1968. 3 August 1961.

PART TWO

LONDON MIDLAND REGION

CHAPTER 15

ST. PANCRAS

St. Pancras station provides an appropriate link with the final picture in the previous chapter and is a good starting point for the London Midland Region to give it its full title.

St. Pancras station was opened on 1 October 1868 and was the culmination of the Bedford to London Extension, thus enabling the Midland Railway to reach its own terminus in the Capital. William Barlow was the designer of the enormous train shed, and the Midland's Grand Hotel, designed by George Gilbert Scott, was not completed until some years later. Now St. Pancras is the gloriously restored terminus for international Eurostar trains.

St. Pancras did not seem to attract the extensive gallery of train observers found at other London termini and I confess my visits to this splendid station were comparatively brief. However, I did record some scenes, which may be of interest here.

Rebuilt 'Royal Scot' 4-6-0 46118 *Royal Welch Fusilier* is bringing the up *Robin Hood* express, 8.15am Nottingham to St. Pancras, into the terminus. 46118 was a Nottingham engine at this date and it lasted until July 1964. 3 January 1961.

Bedford shed's '4MT' 4-6-0 75055 has brought a suburban service from that town to St. Pancras. 75055 is backing out of the terminus over the bridges of Pancras Road, before being serviced for its return journey. Note the now listed gas holders to the right of the picture. 12 September 1959.

Kentish Town's Stanier '4MT' 2-6-4T 42617 is on station pilot duty and waits to take empty stock out of St. Pancras. My brother Chris stands watching, somewhat disconsolately, waiting to go to The Racing Car Show at the New Horticultural Hall. 3 January 1961.

Two days later, St. Pancras was on the agenda again when 'Fairburn' 2-6-4T 42685 was about to take empty stock out of the terminus. The leading vehicle appears to be an ex-LMS corridor coach. 5 January 1961.

St. Pancras station signal box used to be at the platform end until this replacement signal box was opened in 1959. Hardly an inspiring accompaniment to the lovely terminus building. Of interest is an unusual visitor, namely Canklow allocated 'B1' 4-6-0 61334, backing down to the 2.25pm train to Leicester. 5 January 1961.

CHAPTER 16

EUSTON

The Doric Arch, the Great Hall, the elegant curving roof over platforms one and two, nooks and crannies and that infuriating glass screen on the West side of the station, where locomotives would stand anonymously, gave rise to a terminus of enormous character, only to be replaced by a 1960s structure displaying little imagination. Old Euston was opened in 1837 as the London terminus of the London and Birmingham Railway with services to Birmingham commencing in September 1838. Subsequently, the London & North Western Railway, followed by the LMS and British Railways, were the providers of services to the Midlands, North Wales, the Lake District and North-West, Carlisle and over the Border to Scotland. Consequently, locomotives of many varying classes could be seen at the height of steam activity at Euston. It was not the easiest terminus in which to obtain photographs, but there are a few to show now.

The Brownie Box camera wielded by my father produced this atmospheric photograph on 2 August 1930. 'Prince of Wales' class 4-6-0 5675 *Sphinx* is backing empty stock out of platform one under the Ampthill Square bridges. I could not resist including this photograph even though it was not 'in bounds'.

Back to the BR era, 'Princess Royal' pacific 46205 *Princess Victoria* is doing the same as *Sphinx*, in backing empty stock out of Euston's number one platform. 46205 was a Crewe North engine at this time and she was withdrawn at the end of 1961. 5 January 1961.

Longsight based 'Britannia' pacific 70032 *Tennyson* is about to leave Euston with an express for Manchester. The steam cocks have been opened and steam pressure is on the red line. Behind the tender is an ex-LMS brake vehicle. The electric lines for the Watford suburban trains are in the foreground. 12 September 1959.

This is my favourite view of Euston. The superb curving roof above platforms one and two, with both platform roads occupied. On the left, 'Britannia' 4-6-2 70046 just before it was given the name *Anzac* on 2 October 1959. 70046 is a Holyhead engine and presumably it has brought in an express from that direction. At platform one is Edge Hill based 'Royal Scot' 4-6-0 46156 *The South Wales Borderer*, which has brought in a special train from the North-West, burning the smokebox door in the process. 12 September 1959.

CHAPTER 17

HATCH END

Just over thirteen miles out of Euston, Hatch End station had services on the Bakerloo line and electric local services from Euston, as well as having main line platforms. The station opened in August 1842 and was known as Pinner. The name went through a number of variations, settling on Hatch End in 1956. The main line platforms closed in January 1963 and the signal box closure followed in 1964. Worthy of note is that the well-known train timer and author, Cecil J. Allen, moved to Hatch End just before the Second World War. This station provided a most agreeable location to watch trains, whether passenger or freight, and my visit on 31 August 1960 was rewarded with a good variety of locomotives. The day started sunny but became gloomier in the afternoon.

Up trains have a comparatively easy run downhill towards Euston and here grubby '5MT' 4-6-0 45405, based at Bushbury, is making good progress towards the capital with an up express. Note the station sign on the far wall adjacent to platform six.

Rebuilt 'Royal Scot' 4-6-0 46158 *The Loyal Regiment* is enabling the fireman to have a breather as the train rushes towards Euston. The down slow line is signalled for a working and the signal box window is open on this warm August day. 46158 lasted until October 1963.

At last the sun has broken through to illuminate rebuilt 'Royal Scot' 46120 *Royal Inniskilling Fusilier* as it wheels the up *Mancunian* towards Euston at a rate of knots. 46120 was based at Longsight shed, but only briefly. It did have a reputation for rough riding and seemed to be passed round various locomotive depots.

Rugby shed's Stanier '5MT' 4-6-0 44867 is heading a lengthy parcels and van train through Hatch End's up slow line platform. The locomotive is taking it easy in a queue of up trains. Note the bull head rail.

Stanier '8F' 2-8-0 48723 is gently pulling an up mixed freight past Hatch End. The sun makes all the difference and shows up well the signal box and adjacent signals. 48723 lasted virtually until the end of steam in August 1968 and was withdrawn from Lostock Hall shed. Note the Fowler design tender, which does not sit well behind the Stanier cab.

BR '9F' 2-10-0 92153, still carrying a single chimney, is slowly dragging a rake of wagons towards London. Its gentle progress gives the fireman a chance to survey the scene. 92153 is from Toton shed. Note the tidy flowerbeds to the left of the picture.

Unfortunately, the light has become dull as 'Princess Coronation' pacific 46225 *Duchess of Gloucester* rattles the windows as it charges under Hatch End's footbridge with the down afternoon *Caledonian* express. Although in scruffy condition, 46225 is going well past a local audience.

After the excitement of the *Caledonian*, it is back down to earth as '8F' 2-8-0 48370 of Toton shed trundles a lengthy coal train towards London.

A heavy down afternoon express is double headed through Hatch End station. The pilot engine is '5MT' 4-6-0 45078 of Blackpool shed and the train engine is rebuilt 'Patriot' 4-6-0 45530 *Sir Frank Ree* based at Longsight. Manchester would seem to be the destination for this express. Both these locomotives had been withdrawn by the end of 1965.

CHAPTER 18

BETWEEN SKIPTON AND CARLISLE

Tempting as it is to head this chapter 'The Settle and Carlisle Line', I wanted to enlarge the scope of this chapter to include Skipton and some photographs of the Grassington branch. The majority of this chapter's photographs were taken in August 1962 during a family holiday again based at Pateley Bridge in Yorkshire. One exploratory journey took in Westmorland as well, so a picnic lunch near Ais Gill facilitated some train watching. On another day, my brother and I travelled from Skipton to Carlisle, hoping for steam haulage, but a diesel prevailed. A wet afternoon at Carlisle made photography difficult, but in a southbound bay platform sat a 'Black 5' and three ex-LMS coaches. Enquiries revealed that this was the 4.37pm all stations train to Bradford Forster Square, which of course included Skipton. It rained heavily the whole way, but it was a delightful experience, stopping at all the stations to Skipton where we arrived at 7.31pm. Parental anxiety probably reigned, but it was one of those memorable journeys for seeing life and for endurance!

'Crab' 2-6-0 42793 is slowing for Skipton station with a northbound local service. The front coach is a Gresley brake vehicle. Skipton's south signal box is to the left and two water tanks are evident to the right of the locomotive. An ex-LMS brake awaits further work. 6 August 1962.

Carnforth's 'Jubilee' 4-6-0 45625 *Sarawak* enters Skipton station with a train for Leeds City. There is quite an assortment of carriages behind the tender. 16 August 1962.

This is a difficult picture to reproduce, but it shows Stanier '5MT' 4-6-0 44670 after arriving at Skipton with the 4.37pm stopping train from Carlisle. The wet platform reflects the awful weather, which caused the poor light. 9 August 1962.

Bell Busk is situated between Skipton and Hellifield near to the summit of the climb from Skipton. Although out of era, LNWR 'Jumbo' 2-4-0 790 *Hardwicke* double heads Midland 'Compound' 4-4-0 1000 on a special train heading for Carnforth via Settle Junction. 24 April 1976.

On the other side of the River Aire lies Rylstone station on the freight only branch from Skipton to Grassington. This picture is looking towards Skipton. Superb lower quadrant signals offer protection to the level crossing. 16 August 1962.

Beyond Rylstone lies the terminus of the branch at Grassington. Shiny rails reflect the use of the line for freight. The signal box is still in use to operate the splendid gathering of signals protecting the station. 6 August 1962.

A view towards the buffers at Grassington. The station is showing signs of neglect. This station was opened in July 1902 and closed to passengers in September 1930, but lasted until August 1969 for freight traffic. The site is now a residential estate. 6 August 1962.

This scene is taken from Shotlock Hill tunnel just before Ais Gill summit, where Wild Boar Fell oversees the landscape and before the railway drops downhill through Mallerstang. A northbound mixed freight is making its leisurely way towards Ais Gill, the locomotive being Caprotti 'Black 5' 4-6-0 44753. 17 August 1962.

A little nearer Ais Gill summit was a pleasant lay-by on the B6259 road, a few hundred yards north of the previous location. 'Britannia' pacific 70052 *Firth of Tay*, a Corkerhill engine at this time, makes rapid progress with an up express. The leading coach is of Thompson design. 17 August 1962.

At the same location, 'Jubilee' 4-6-0 45659 *Drake,* from Leeds Holbeck, is wheeling a lengthy freight away from Ais Gill summit. The driver is watching the photographer closely. Note the low run of telegraph poles. 17 August 1962.

An occupation bridge at Ais Gill summit provides a view of 'WD' 2-8-0 90389 coming up the hill without too much fuss as it heads a freight southwards. 17 August 1962.

Turn to face south and 90389 is about to pass Ais Gill signal box, 1,169 feet above sea level. The upper quadrant signal is showing a clear route. The Ais Gill northbound starter signal is prominent, as is the telegraph pole route. This signal box was brought into use in April 1890 and was closed in January 1981 and was subsequently preserved at the Midland Railway Centre, Butterley. 17 August 1962.

Moving to the north of Ais Gill summit, we see the struggle that epitomises the work of the Settle to Carlisle line as Stanier '8F' 2-8-0 48708 blasts up to the summit with what looks like an anhydrite train from Long Meg sidings. The locomotive's exhaust is almost being carried before it by the breeze. 48708 lasted until April 1967. 17 August 1962.

At Carlisle, the rain is heavy and so are the locomotives! 'Princess Coronation' pacific 46235 *City of Birmingham,* from Crewe North shed, is waiting to back on to an up express. 46235 is preserved in the Birmingham Science Museum. 9 August 1962.

'Princess Royal' 4-6-2 46201 *Princess Elizabeth* is backing down to the stock of a Perth express, at Carlisle. 46201 was shedded at Upperby at this date. A Fowler '4MT' 2-6-4T '42301' is behind 46201's tender. Thankfully, 46201 is preserved and is currently awaiting repair work for a return to the main line. 9 August 1962.

Rebuilt 'Royal Scot' 46103 *Royal Scots Fusilier* has the route set by a 'dolly' shunt signal as it reverses through Carlisle station. 46103 was based at Carlisle Upperby from June to September 1962 and was withdrawn by the end of 1962. 9 August 1962.

In almost the same place as 46103 is 'Britannia' 4-6-2 70038 *Robin Hood*, bereft of nameplates and far away from its original East Anglian haunts. Shedded at Carlisle Kingmoor, 70038 awaits its next duty. It has about a year of life left, being withdrawn in August 1967. 29 July 1966.

CHAPTER 19

CUMBRIAN COAST

I n late Summer 1962, I had a brief activity holiday based at St. Bees School, on the Cumbrian Coast. In between assemblies, energetic hill walks and climbing Scafell Pike, I found that the Cumbrian Coast railway line was in distant view from the school grounds. Once 'Patriot' 4-6-0 45550 had passed the grounds, I managed to get leave to visit the 'Ratty', the Ravenglass and Eskdale Railway, in order to see what was on offer on the Cumbrian Coast line. As usual, I had to economise on film, but some photographs are available from that holiday. On the outward journey from Euston to St. Bees on 24 August 1962, 'Princess Coronation' pacific 46239 *City of Chester* took us to Lancaster. Ivatt '4MT' 2-6-0 43004 completed the journey to St. Bees. On the return to London, two 'Jubilees', 45617 *Mauritius* and 45633 *Aden,* managed the train from Barrow to Lancaster and 45633 took us on to Preston. I do not have notes for the rest of the journey. Here are some local pictures taken during the holiday.

The first visit to the R&ER found *River Esk* on duty and here the fifteen inch gauge Davey Paxman built 2-8-2 is backing on to its train at Ravenglass. The cylinder steam cocks are in operation, before the start of the journey to Dalegarth. Ivatt '4MT' 43004 was the motive power for the return to St. Bees. 30 August 1962.

A brief interlude at Bootle before returning to Ravenglass for a second R&ER visit. 'Jubilee' 4-6-0 45674 *Duncan* is slowing for the Bootle stop with a train for Barrow. 45674 was based at Crewe North at this date. The lower quadrant signal for Bootle station can just be seen to the left of the picture. 1 September 1962.

Whilst waiting for the return train from Ravenglass to St. Bees, 'Jubilee' 4-6-0 45629 *Straits Settlements* is heading a southbound freight, passing the up waiting shelter at Ravenglass station. 1 September 1962.

This photograph had to be taken in a hurry, having alighted from this train at St. Bees. Crewe North allocated 'Jubilee' 4-6-0 45552 *Silver Jubilee* was motive power from Ravenglass to St. Bees and here 45552 is departing the latter station. Note the raised numerals on the cab side, with only the 52 cleaned. The train of ex-LMS coaches was destined for Workington. 1 September 1962.

CHAPTER 20

MARYLEBONE TO LEICESTER CENTRAL

By early 1963 it was clear that the main line that once formed part of the core of the Great Central Railway was being deliberately run down, certainly from a passenger carrying point of view. Passenger traffic to the Great Central London terminus of Marylebone commenced on 15 March 1899. A new line had been built from Nottingham to meet the existing Metropolitan Railway at Quainton Road station where the line towards London became the Metropolitan and Great Central Joint Railway. At the 1923 Grouping, the line became part of the LNER and in 1948, on Nationalisation, part of the BR Eastern Region, but in 1958 it was transferred to the London Midland Region. At the beginning of 1960, the express services to London, such as *The South Yorkshireman* and *The Master Cutler*, were withdrawn and the service to London reduced to three daily semi-fast trains each way. The final curtain came for steam services into Marylebone in September 1966. Happily, Marylebone thrives as a terminus today for Chiltern Railways, but the line with its Berne loading gauge could have been a superb main line national asset.

On a gloomy January day, Stanier '5MT' 4-6-0 45215 has arrived at Marylebone with the 8.15am train from Nottingham. The external condition of the locomotive speaks volumes. The crew members were probably thankful to have arrived. 25 January 1964.

On an earlier occasion, I had an opportunity to see some steam before starting work in September 1963. The once glorious Great Central Railway was a prime target and at the Marylebone terminus is rebuilt 'Royal Scot' 4-6-0 46163 *Civil Service Rifleman* having arrived with the 8.15am Nottingham to Marylebone semi-fast service. 46163 was allocated to Annesley shed as displayed by the chalked shed code. 16 July 1963.

Harrow-on-the-Hill station is just over nine miles from Marylebone. The Metropolitan Line of London Transport had an intensive service via this station from London to Amersham, and the BR trains to and from Marylebone were interspersed with these services. Here standard '4MT' 2-6-0 76041, based at Cricklewood, is heading a lightweight freight, probably bound for Quainton yard. 16 July 1963.

Annesley's rebuilt 'Royal Scot' 4-6-0 46163 *Civil Service Rifleman* is bringing the 8.15am train from Nottingham into the Art-Deco style Harrow-on-the-Hill station. 16 July 1963.

Another Stanier
'5MT' 4-6-0
45262 is moving
empty stock out of
Marylebone. Gloom
and dirt contrive to
hide detail, but the
atmosphere is there.
45262 surprisingly
lasted until August
1968. 25 January
1964.

In January 1964, Stanier '5MT' 4-6-0 45215 is following in 46163's tracks as it brings the 8.15am from
Nottingham into Harrow-on-the-Hill. At least there is another intending passenger other than the author.
25 January 1964.

Moving northwards, the disused Waddesdon station in Buckinghamshire provides a useful lineside location. Cricklewood's '4MT' 2-6-0 76035 is taking a down freight to the yards at Quainton station. 6 August 1963.

Waddesdon station looking north as Stanier '5MT' 4-6-0 45215 passes through, light engine. Waddesdon railway station was opened by the Metropolitan Railway in January 1897 and closed in July 1936 when the 'Met' services were cut back to Aylesbury. 6 August 1963.

Willesden's 'Britannia' pacific 70033 *Charles Dickens* is in charge of the 2.38pm Marylebone to Nottingham train at Waddesdon. The 43 milepost confirms the location. The road bridge carries a lane accessing Quainton and Waddesdon villages. 6 August 1963.

Standard '5MT' 4-6-0 73010, belonging to Woodford Halse shed, puts on a good show as it rapidly heads north with the 4.38pm train for Nottingham. 6 August 1963.

A Metropolitan and Great Central Joint Railway trespassers notice at Quainton Road station.
6 August 1963.

Quainton Road station officially opened on 30 November 1896 and closed completely on 4 July 1966. It was at one time the terminus for the Brill Tramway, which ceased working on 30 November 1935. Here is the deserted station looking north.
6 August 1963.

Quainton Road station looking south towards Waddesdon. Note the lower quadrant signals, goods wagons aplenty and the signal box with the appropriate name board. The station and yards now form part of the Buckinghamshire Railway Centre. 6 August 1963.

The next location on this journey is Leicester Central station, which opened in March 1899, only to be closed to passengers in June 1969 after the gradual run-down of services from 1960 onwards. This and the remaining pictures at Leicester Central were taken on 31 July 1963. I had travelled from Marylebone on the 8.38am DMU to Leicester to make the most of this visit, but still wonder to this day whether I should have waited for the 2.38pm service which was 'Royal Scot' hauled … hindsight! However, here is 'Royal Scot' 4-6-0 46111 *Royal Fusilier* after depositing a van in the bay platform. 46111 would continue south on a parcels train, which is waiting in the up platform. 46111's friendly driver is watching the camera.

Next on the scene was Annesley's Stanier '8F' 48024 with a heavy southbound mixed freight. Note the water tank in the yard to the right of the picture.

BR '9F' 2-10-0s were well known for their efforts with the Annesley to Woodford Halse 'windcutter' coal trains. Here 92032 heads south through the station with a rake of coal wagons.

Stanier '5MT' 4-6-0
44848 is bringing
ex-LMS empty stock
from the north into
Leicester Central
station and passing
the Great Central
Hotel in the process.
44848 is shedded
locally and worked
until February 1968.

The 2.38pm semi-fast from Marylebone has reached Leicester Central behind 'Royal Scot' 4-6-0 46112
Sherwood Forester although nameplates seem to be absent. The signal gantry is on West Bridge Viaduct over
the River Soar.

It was a pleasure to see ex-LNER motive power on the Great Central! Here York shed's 'V2' 2-6-2 60941 is heading north with a fitted freight, making shadowy reflections along Leicester Central's platform five.

Time to head for home. 'Britannia' 4-6-2 70012 *John of Gaunt* is at the head of the 5-15pm Nottingham to Marylebone train as passengers board and post sacks are loaded. My notes record a "good run" back to the Capital. 70012 was Willesden shedded and was withdrawn in December 1967.

CHAPTER 21

NORTH WALES

Very fortunately, a pal and I decided to take a week's holiday in Wales to cover as much of the ex-Great Western lines and the ex-LMS lines as possible. The Great Western coverage is portrayed in my *Southern and Western* book and this chapter will deal with matters London Midland to give it the full title. In the short time available, we managed main and branch line travel as well as shed visits. We were just in time as some of the haulage locomotives were withdrawn shortly after our visit. The railway between Chester and Holyhead was built as a fast running main line railway to cope with holiday and ferry traffic to Ireland. Two notable structures were needed to carry the railway and the Stephenson tubular bridges at Conway and Menai Bridge fulfilled that purpose, the trains being carried within the bridge tubes. Whilst parts of the line had been in use from 1848, the complete route was opened by October 1850 once the two tubular bridges had been finished. The LNWR was responsible for train services initially, succeeded by the LMS and BR, which is when we look at the area.

It is not clear how we reached Bangor from Beddgelert, but here Chester shed's Stanier '5MT' 4-6-0 45419 poses for the camera at Bangor shed on 7 June 1964.

Bangor shed was very close to the station, so it seemed appropriate to make a visit. Resident Stanier '4MT' 2-6-4T 42489 is on shed. Note Bangor West End signal box in the distance behind 42489. 7 June 1964.

BR Standard '2MT' 2-6-0 78003 is adding to the atmosphere at Bangor shed. Behind 78003 is '5MT' 45345, and 2-6-4T 42489 is alongside. 7 June 1964.

Bangor resident Ivatt '2MT' 2-6-2T 41234 is ready for duty, which may well be the freight on the Amlwch branch. Bangor shed closed to steam in October 1966. 7 June 1964.

On the following day, a bus took us to Portmadoc where BR standard '3MT' 2-6-2T 82000 provided motive power to Afon Wen. A DMU was expected for the journey to Bangor, but by good fortune there was steam substitution, with Bangor shed's Stanier '5MT' 4-6-0 45223 heading a push-pull rake of coaches, tender first. 45223 can be seen here, en route, through the motor coach 'cab end' window. The Afon Wen branch closed in December 1964. 8 June 1964.

Nearing Caernarvon station, we pass Fairburn '4MT' 2-6-4T 42074 of Bangor shed. 42074 is standing in the goods depot sidings and the crew is much amused by the passing of 45223, with the train from Afon Wen. 8 June 1964.

Stanier '5MT' 4-6-0 45276, of Stoke shed, provided motive power to Llandudno Junction station from Bangor, whilst hauling a Manchester bound train. 8 June 1964.

Llandudno Junction shed could not be missed with its variety of motive power. 'Jinty' 0-6-0T 47361 is in charge of a solitary wagon outside the shed. 8 June 1964.

Alongside the 'Jinty', a Stanier '5MT' 4-6-0 45282 is being guided into the shed by a shunter hanging precariously from the tender handrail. 45282 would be active until May 1968. 8 June 1964.

Outside the shed, '4F' 0-6-0 44389 is in steam awaiting its next turn. The tender is well filled with coal and note the tender cab to give the crew protection for tender first working. 8 June 1964.

Looking woebegone and out of steam, 'Britannia' 4-6-2 70044 *Earl Haig* is resting on one of the shed sidings.
It was a Crewe North engine and lasted until October 1966. 8 June 1964.

Clearly these two locomotives have been put into store as their chimneys are sacked to keep out the elements.
'4F' 0-6-0 44525 looks quite tidy and survived until September 1966. The second locomotive is believed to be
'2MT' 2-6-2T 84025. Llandudno Junction shed closed to steam on 3 October 1966. 8 June 1964.

Back at Llandudno Junction station, 'Britannia' pacific 70018 *Flying Dutchman* awaits departure to Holyhead. 70018 is allocated to Crewe North and was once a Western Region engine as evidenced by the handholds cut into the smoke deflectors. 8 June 1964.

I was on the wrong platform to catch 'Jubilee' 4-6-0 45657 *Tyrwhitt* from Patricroft shed as the locomotive slowly heads freight westwards. Withdrawal would be in just over three months. 8 June 1964.

Stanier '5MT' 4-6-0 44661 of Llandudno Junction shed stands ready for departure at the Llandudno terminus station. This was the nearest thing to sunshine all day, but at least it was dry. 44661 returned us to Llandudno Junction station. 8 June 1964.

Dull day, dirty engine, but the drawbacks were overcome by the presence of 'Princess Coronation' pacific 46254 *City of Stoke-on-Trent* as it waits to leave Rhyl for Chester. It had wheeled our train up to 75mph between Colwyn Bay and Abergele. 8 June 1964.

Here 46254 provides an imposing image as it leaves Rhyl for Chester under a curious overhead signal gantry. Three months later 46254 would be no more. 8 June 1964.

For the return run to Llandudno Junction, the motive power was rebuilt 'Royal Scot' 4-6-0 46148 *The Manchester Regiment* with eleven coaches in tow. The driver was the same man as on 46254 and he was enthusiastic about the two classes of locomotive. 46148 is at Llandudno Junction waiting to leave for Holyhead where it was based. 46148 alternated between Llandudno Junction and Holyhead sheds between September 1962 and November 1964 when it was withdrawn. 8 June 1964.

9 June 1964 dawned dull and very wet. The plan was to travel to Llanberis station to see if there was any activity. The next six pictures will reflect the events of that morning. On arrival at the station, the thrice weekly freight was in evidence as standard '2MT' 2-6-0 78032 was shunting wagons in the pouring rain. The nine mile branch from Caernarvon opened in July 1869.

After much persuasion, the guard allowed us to ride in the brake van of the pick-up freight to Menai Bridge station. The brake van made an excellent photographic platform as the train departed Llanberis station.

The next station, Cwm-y-Glo, stands forlornly in the rain.

Pontrhythallt was passed next, its very short platform supporting the local coal merchant's Morris Commercial lorry.

A view from the guard's van of the wagons and 78032 making progress along the branch towards Caernarvon. The main freight traffic was coal.

78032 and wagons curve downhill towards Caernarvon station. The branch to Llanberis closed to freight and excursion traffic in September 1964, three months after this brake van ride. Regular passenger trains had ceased in 1930.

The weather had improved on 10 June 1964 for a visit to the Amlwch branch from Gaerwen. The seventeen mile journey was DMU powered, but en-route the daily freight was passed at Llangefni as Bangor's Ivatt '2MT' 2-6-2T 41234 was shunting wagons in the yard. Part of the open ground frame is visible on the right.

At Amlwch station, the DMU has departed and its place has been taken by 41234 alongside the ticket collector's office. The goods warehouse is to the right of the engine.

Peace returns to Amlwch station and all looks well with the world. The branch was opened in March 1865 and became a passenger traffic casualty in December 1964.

On the final day in North Wales, another trip to Holyhead was the plan. Stanier '5MT' 4-6-0 45045 was at the head of the train in sunshine at Rhyl, but by Bangor the clouds were back. Here is 45045 at Bangor just before departure for Holyhead. 12 June 1964.

By afternoon, it was raining again, but rebuilt 'Patriot' 4-6-0 45530 *Sir Frank Ree* stands proudly at Holyhead station with an afternoon express, probably a London train. 45530 was shedded at Willesden at this date. 12 June 1964.

45530 is about to plunge into the tube forming the Britannia Bridge over the Menai Strait. Note the lions above the train and to the right. 12 June 1964.

Farewell to North Wales as 'Patriot' 45530 heads away from Bangor station and is about to enter the Eastern tunnel under Bangor Mountain. Light can be seen at the far end of the tunnel. 45530 was handled well in awful weather conditions. 12 June 1964.

CHAPTER 22

HELLIFIELD, 30 JULY 1967

By 1967, motor cars had begun to submerge our railway interest, especially as steam was in retreat and it had become hard to watch the neglect of much loved locomotives. On a fortnight's tour of England and Scotland in a 1932 Austin 20 Limousine, our return route took us via Hellifield, where on Saturday, 30 July 1967, we visited the station to watch the action and the shed, where various preserved locomotives were housed including 'A4' 60010 *Dominion of Canada*, 'V2' 4771 *Green Arrow* and Midland Railway 4-2-2 118. Hellifield new station was opened by the Midland Railway in June 1880, once the Lancashire and Yorkshire Railway had completed the line from Blackburn. Hellifield today is a watering point for steam excursions north and southbound, unfortunately with no station access for such excursion passengers.

Stanier '5MT' 4-6-0 44761, from Springs Branch shed, is bringing its southbound freight to a halt at Hellifield, passing the closed locomotive shed in the process.

Standard '4MT' 4-6-0 75019 is stopping the pick-up freight to enable the crew to refill what looks like an enormous tea can. The weather, as usual, is dull and damp.

Kingmoor's '5MT' 4-6-0 45481 is making a vigorous getaway from Hellifield with a northbound special train off the Blackburn line, perhaps a seaside excursion.

This grimy 'Black 5' 44866 is from Trafford Park and is awaiting the 'rightaway' to head north with another special, hard on the heels of 45481.

Carnforth shed's '5MT' 4-6-0 44987 is heading a southbound local train. 44987's numberplate shows the type of embellishment expected from a Scottish 'Black 5' perhaps.

It was not the best place to catch 'Jubilee' 4-6-0 45593 *Kolhapur* as it races north with the 10.17am Leeds to Carlisle express, but it was what we wanted to see. 45593 was withdrawn in October 1967 and is thankfully still with us.

To return to the motoring theme just briefly, 1932 Austin 20 Limousine BMH 570 is about to enter Yorkshire on the way south from Hellifield, no doubt via an obscure route! Four of us had paid £5 each for the use of this vehicle and the grand old machine had reliably carried us for 2,000 miles round England and Scotland. 30 July 1967.

CHAPTER 23

BARRY ISLAND

After the Hellifield visit, it was clear that the demise of steam was imminent. Following the final steam specials in August 1968, Barry Island steam scrapyard was visited on 14 September 1968, which at this time had the atmosphere of a graveyard devoid of hope. We did not know then that this yard was to be the source of renewal for UK steam. The story is well known now.

Stanier 'Mogul' 42968 looks very forlorn at Barry Island. Happily, this engine is preserved at the Severn Valley Railway.

Another sad scene depicts 'Crab' 2-6-0 42765, but all is not lost as this locomotive is gloriously turned out in LMS Crimson Lake livery as 13065 at the East Lancashire Railway.

CHAPTER 24

RENAISSANCE

This is not a book about preservation, but to present a positive picture after the apparent gloom of Barry Island, here are two photographs from a visit to Steamtown Carnforth on 6 September 1970. At the time there were five Stanier 'Black 5's, two Fairburn '4MT' 2-6-4Ts, one 'B1' 4-6-0 and an Ivatt '2MT' 2-6-0 in the shed, all in the process of restoration and waiting for new and fulfilling futures.

Stanier 'Black 5' 4-6-0 5231, with LMS style numberplate, already looks capable of work. It subsequently appeared on various preserved lines including the Nene Valley Railway and the North Yorkshire Moors Railway, as well as working extensively on the main line. It now carries the name *The Sherwood Forester*.

Given the title of this book, it was satisfying to record locomotives from both regions under the Carnforth roof. 'B1' 4-6-0 61306 is safe and dry and it would not be too long before it returned to the main line in apple green livery. Floreat Vapor.